THE TEENAGE

UNDERSTANDING

18–20 year olds

Beta Copley
and
Gianna Williams

of

THE TAVISTOCK CLINIC

Series Editor: Elsie Osborne

ROSEN DALE PRESS

ROSENDALE PRESS

First published in Great Britain in 1995 by:
Rosendale Press Ltd
Premier House, 10 Greycoat Place
London SW1P 1SB

Design by Pep Reiff

Typeset by Ace Filmsetting Ltd
Printed in the United Kingdom by The Cromwell Press

British Library Cataloguing in Publication Data
A catalogue record for this book is available from
The British Library

ISBN 1 872803 80 6

The Tavistock Clinic, London, was founded in 1920, in order to meet the needs of people whose lives had been disrupted by the First World War. Today, it is still committed to understanding people's needs though, of course, times and people have changed. Now, as well as working with adults and adolescents, the Tavistock Clinic has a large department for children and families. This offers help to parents who are finding the challenging task of bringing up their children daunting and has, therefore, a wide experience of children of all ages. It is firmly committed to early intervention in the inevitable problems that arise as children grow up, and to the view that if difficulties are caught early enough, parents are the best people to help their children with them.

Professional Staff of the Clinic were, therefore, pleased to be able to contribute to this series of books to describe the ordinary development of children, to help in spotting the growing pains and to provide ways that parents might think about their children's growth.

THE AUTHORS

Beta Copley has worked and taught for many years at the Tavistock Clinic. She is co-author with Barbara Forryan of *Therapeutic Work with Children and Young People* (1987, Robert Royce) and is author of *The World of Adolescence: Literature, Society and Psychoanalytic Psychotherapy* (1983, Free Association Books). She is married with 2 children and 3 grandchildren.

Gianna Williams is a Consultant Psychotherapist in the Adolescent Department of the Tavistock Clinic, and is course tutor of the postgraduate Diploma/MA in Psychoanalytic Observational Studies (Tavistock/University of East London). She is co-author with Isca Wittenberg and Elsie Osborne of *The Emotional Experience of Learning and Teaching* (1983, Routledge) and has published numerous articles relating to adolescence including the topics of eating disorders, groups and gangs and psychotherapeutic work with ethnic minorities. She is married with 2 children and 1 grandchild.

CONTENTS

INTRODUCTION

This, the last book in a series concerned with the development of young people, describes a milestone in their lives. The teenager is now allowed to vote and is treated as a responsible adult. At a time in life when young people are involved in making important choices, many are still busy finding out about themselves and who they really feel themselves to be. It is within these years that a sense of who one is often becomes clearer and more definable in terms of: '*I* am' or '*I* think that . . .'

For many young people and their parents this period will represent the beginning of the end of family life as they have known it. Some young people may leave home in order to pursue further education. Some may take up work away from their parents' home and some may wish to set up a new home either with friends or with a partner.

In earlier years the family provided the central emotional focus and a holding function which was later, at least partly, replaced by the feeling of belonging to a peer group of young people. In the age group which we are now discussing, a firmer sense of individual identity, often accompanied by an increasingly intimate long-term relationship with a partner begins to develop. In other words, young people are becoming more adult.

Being able to move on from the centrality of the family and peer group world and take direct responsibility for how one leads one's own life, is likely to be the outcome of a gradual process of growing up. Development, however, can be very uneven and someone who is, in age, a young adult, may at times be uncertain on his or her own feet and feel in need of support. This is in particular the case when there is a wish to move forward without yet really having found firm ground upon which to stand.

This is also a radical time of change for parents. The departure of the first child from home, and even more so of the last one, turns a new page in the book of their lives. Difficult and fraught as the relationship between parents and their adolescent children may at times have been, the moment of a young person's departure is likely to evoke painful feelings and can be a watershed in the lives of parents as well as their children, who can leave an empty space when they go.

The experience demands an adjustment within the parents themselves, whether they are together as a couple, separated or single. Even parents who are very supportive of their children's development, and by no means overprotective, may worry about the capacity of their teenagers to manage adequately in their new environment. This natural worry is all the greater if the parents feel that the departure has not been sufficiently thought through, and may leave them perplexed as to whether and how they may be able to help. Some parents may need to make decisions, which they may experience as difficult ones, about the direction their lives are going to take once the children have left. In particular, some may have to relate not only to feelings of loss of their children as children, but also to a feeling of loss of purposefulness in their own lives. This is indeed a time when substantial adjustments to change may need to take place in both generations.

Throughout the book we provide illustrations of events of a kind which may occur for young people and their parents at this time in their lives. These are based on many years of professional experience but, in order to respect confidentiality, are not direct representations of particular individuals.

CHAPTER ONE

THE BOUNDARY OF ADULTHOOD AND A GROWING SENSE OF SELF

Learning to know oneself

Between the ages of eighteen and twenty young people tend to develop a greater capacity to form their own opinions and become clearer about their own personal aspirations and tastes.

Jenny, now aged eighteen, used to wear very torn and frayed jeans and undone shoelaces on her trainers. She was aware that her father found this very provocative, especially when other relatives of his generation were present. He had, on one occasion, refused to take Jenny on a family outing, saying that he was ashamed of how she was dressed. Jenny, on the other hand, had felt both offended and uncomprehending of her father's reaction.

Jenny is now taking a business course and wears neat and clean jeans. She feels that this change is part of a natural development in herself and not an outcome of parental disapproval. Father himself is aware of this and has come to understand Jenny's dislike of changes in herself being seen as a climb-down or the consequence of being told off. Jenny, however, can now laugh a little when reminded how the torn jeans used to upset Auntie Gladys. Her sense of identity is now more secure and she does not need to bolster it by showing her relatives how different she is from them. She also seems to take some pleasure in her new appearance. The heat of the early adolescent years appears to have simmered down.

When a little younger, Jenny used to be very conforming to the taste of her group of friends, not only in her appearance – indeed they all used to wear torn jeans and have undone shoelaces – but also in her allegiance to the type of music approved of by the others. Now that she is eighteen, she appears to have developed a much more personal taste. She has become more adventurous in buying tapes of pop music which she really likes, but would have frowned upon in the past because they were not 'in' with her friends. Jenny also occasionally borrows one of her older brother's opera tapes. She has acquired a new freedom to be herself.

Jenny's brother Bob, now twenty, used to irritate his parents by leaving tabloid newspapers around which he knew could be offensive to them. At this time he was not really aligned with the political and social contents of the papers he bought but followed the latest trend shared by his current group of friends. Picking a fight with his parents was not only provocative, but included a wish, through confrontation, to become clearer about his own political and social standards. Between eighteen and twenty he has developed a genuine interest in some social and political issues, and, instead of seeking ready-made responses from the minds of his group of friends, he can openly express feelings of doubt and worry about the rights and wrongs regarding national and international issues, such as those of war, nuclear power and social benefits.

Both Jenny and Bob have a better sense of what they actually feel and want as individuals without having to assert themselves in opposition to their parents. This shift contributes significantly to an easing of family life. It will also help Jenny and Bob to develop a more friendly and helpful picture of parents in their minds. A benevolent inner presence of this kind generates a feeling of having enhanced resources and a better sense of being a person with a firm central core. The sense of having good internal support is particularly relevant and valuable when major changes are taking place and important decisions need to be taken.

The feeling of becoming more firmly oneself both contributes to, and is contributed to, by other factors. These include forming a working identity, the quality of a relationship which one can establish with a partner, and, in some cases undertaking further studies. We discuss such issues in the following chapters.

CHAPTER TWO

WHAT SHALL I DO NEXT? THE DEVELOPMENT OF A WORKING IDENTITY

Children are often asked "what are you going to be when you are grown-up?". Parents may not often be asked what they have in mind, but may well have a variety of images relating to what they would like their children to be or become in the future. In some cases they may hope their children will follow in their own footsteps in their choice of study or work; in other cases they may want him or her to achieve something that they have not been able to fulfil themselves. Such feelings are natural and shared by many. It is important, nevertheless, for parents to help their children to find their own idiom and feel free to develop so that they are most of all true to themselves. Choosing a very different occupation or even lifestyle from that of one's parents need not be anti-parental. We shall shortly see, in the examples of Yvonne and Roy, that young people can also find inspiration for defining their working identity in their relationship with a teacher or an admired relative.

It may be helpful for a parent to be aware, or perhaps recall, that the crucial moment of embarking on a new project can be a time of turmoil and anxiety. Some degree of upheaval is natural whenever important decisions have to be made, even if they are not final. First jobs or initial choice of further studies do not necessarily involve a life commitment; changes often follow. Painful feelings of doubt and uncertainty can be avoided by taking the short cut of slotting into a pre-existing groove, but this could constrict the unfolding of different facets of the young person's genuine identity.

At times an unthinking way to avoid anxiety takes the shape of a negative choice, such as the son of an engineer deciding that he will be anything but an engineer. This could be a way, although not a very constructive one, to diminish the impact of a daunting range of possibilities. However at the age of eighteen some adolescents may still not find it easy to say "I am myself" without saying "I am not you".

Making a career choice

Gavin's father was a general practitioner and he and his wife would have liked to see Gavin following in his father's footsteps, and, perhaps, even going further in his career by becoming a successful specialist. Gavin, in spite of some rebelliousness in the early years of his adolescence, was successful in his studies and, on the whole, had a good relationship with his father. He knew his father would understand and bear his own disappointment if he did not go into medicine. He chose a University course which could lead to his becoming a teacher. One of the qualities he admired in his father was his concern for his patients. Although he did not choose to enter his father's profession, he carried an admired quality of father inside himself which could be given expression in his own work. Gavin, at nineteen, seemed to be well on the path of developing a genuine identity of his own, related to qualities he admired in both parents, but in no way imitative of them.

Yvonne's parents both worked in a small horticultural business. They could have used their daughter's help and there would also have been room for some fresh initiative by her in the business. Yvonne herself enjoyed the beauty of the flowers, but did not feel attracted by the prospect of this kind of work. She was very fond of music and decided to take up a musical training and continue the study of an instrument which she was already playing at school, where she had been well taught and encouraged by a good teacher. Her parents had hoped that she would join them, but they knew their daughter very well and realized that she was making a genuine choice which would enable her to have a fuller life. Although disappointed, they were quite prepared to accept that she did not want to fit into their ready-made slot.

The meaning of work

Roy, aged nineteen, had developed, on the whole, a good sense of himself by his late teens. His working identity was very central to him. He was already a skilled motor mechanic and was now earning good money. As well as working in a garage he had put advertisements in the local paper in order to explore ways of increasing his income. He had been interested in cars and engines since childhood. He had, for example, at times been quite spellbound by his young uncle Daren's skill in taking the engine of his motor bike to pieces, oiling and greasing the parts and then putting the engine together again.

Roy was fortunate in that he had very clear ideas about the type of work which would give him a great deal of job satisfaction. He was also able to get suitable employment. In addition he also went to evening classes. He earned little at first, but had a strong drive to be self-sufficient.

The problems of unemployment

Some young people look for a job after leaving school without a very specific focus apart from that of earning a living. Even when the work in itself is not particularly rewarding, it can represent a source of new relationships or even friendships. Work in addition provides a feeling of really belonging to adult society. There is a considerable contrast between young people who are unable to obtain work and those, such as Roy, who, on leaving school have been fortunate enough to find what they felt was reasonable employment, and able to establish a clear working identity. The social life of those not working is depleted by lack of financial resources as well as low morale. Lack of work can thus be a threat to a young person's feeling of growing up with a real sense of becoming adult.

Beverley had not liked her years at school very much and, when she left, had neither formal qualifications nor any specific interests. She obtained a temporary cleaning job in a school for a few months, but lost this when the regular worker returned from maternity leave. After that a period of unemployment was followed by a youth training scheme which she did not enjoy. By eighteen she was living at home and she accepted in a very half-hearted manner a low paid part-time job – the only one she could find. The pay was lower than a benefit level of income, but she had been faced with a truly grim choice between unemployment or work which she perceived as exploitation. Beverley's parents agreed that Beverley should take any job available, whatever the pay. Beverley herself was extremely resentful about the pressure she felt under to take on just any job. She became morose and lacking in self-esteem, feeling that there was no place she could take up in the working world which could give her any real sense of achievement.

Even when Beverley did have some money to spare for going out, she did not like to mix with her old friends in the pub because she felt that they would look down on her. She did, however, keep going to the job centre and eventually found a better job as a shop assistant. She had not had much opportunity to move away and felt resentful about still being at home. It was, therefore, one of the reliefs of having a salary that she was now able to contribute more to the housekeeping. She felt better in herself, was able to go out more, and the quality of her social life improved.

Beverley was in quite low spirits for a considerable time but was able to recover. Things did not turn out so well for some of Beverley's school friends who could not find a job or later became unemployed. One of them, Harry, was a fairly cheerful lad when he was sixteen. He was very good at sport, particularly football. He left with a few G.C.S.E.s but no clear idea about what work he might want to do. However, no employment at all was forthcoming. He was included in a training scheme which he found lacking in purpose and unable to stimulate any interest in him. Although he continued to practice in the local football team and maintained some social contact, he had no money to go out, even at week-ends. At eighteen, in an effort to find work, he moved to the house of an uncle and aunt who lived in a town where he thought he would have a better chance of employment. His hopes were sadly not fulfilled. By the time he was nearly nineteen he spent most of his time watching television in an isolated and morose frame of mind. Although he missed his football, he was too dispirited to try to join a local club. His low spirits led him to become listless and insensitive to his personal appearance. His aunt and uncle also became irritated by him and made it clear that he had outstayed his welcome. Harry felt very defeated, returned home for only two weeks and then decided to move to London, again in the hope of finding some prospects of work. He had not realized that having no fixed address would make his project more difficult. He joined the ranks of the many homeless and unemployed people in the capital.

Harry's run-down appearance and negative feelings about himself bore very little resemblance to those of the springy football player of his school years, when he was often given the nickname of a current football hero. At that time, Harry's achievement in sport contributed to his sense of purpose and identity. This was lost in his years of unemployment.

Adverse external circumstances, as shown in the examples of Beverley and Harry, can indeed hinder the development of a working identity and depress self esteem and drive.

CHAPTER THREE

LEAVING HOME

Starting work may often involve a young person in living away from home. Leaving home at this age usually has a different quality and meaning from the precipitate departure of a younger teenager, which may well be motivated by some degree of unhappiness. For older ones, leaving home can, on the contrary, represent a measure of their capacity to be independent.

Living with other young people

Some kinds of training, such as nursing, may provide residential accommodation, but most young people who take a job away from home will have to find their own place to live. The experience of everyday living with others in hostels or halls of residence, or where there is any form of shared accommodation, may provide an unintended opportunity of getting to know some less desirable aspects of oneself. Working girls frequently join in a flat-share at this age, and the experience of housekeeping and financial management involved may represent an initial step towards becoming autonomous.

Although the fact of living away from home is often perceived as an achievement and an exciting experience, it is not devoid of problems and anxieties. We have to remember that, even at this age, surprising though it may be to the young person, there is still a child within who may find separation difficult, albeit attractive. As Laura discovered, parents may, at times, be more long-suffering than contemporaries.

Laura, aged nineteen, had excelled at domestic science and home economics at school and was now working her way up to becoming a buyer in a multiple store. She used to frown on her mother's standards of housekeeping, believing that she herself could do a great deal better. She had been keen to join in a flat-share, but was surprised when she encountered some difficulties in her relationships with the other girls. They had agreed to Laura bringing her cat, but problems arose. Sally, one of the girls, sat down to have a cup of tea in front of the television just before going out in her smart new black outfit for a date, and got extremely angry when she found her skirt was covered in cat's hair. Sally swore at Laura, telling her that for all her flaunting of great housekeeping qualities, she was a mess to live with: she could not even clean up after her cat when it messed the chairs and did not wash up the cat's plate, so that the flat smelt of cat food. Laura, feeling very hurt, was almost tempted to return home. The gradual resolution of this conflict, however, helped her to learn from bitter experience. She had to face that she was not automatically a super housewife, and that there was a little girl in her somewhere, who took it for granted that there would still be a mother around who would clear up after her.

The presence of the child in the adult

Laura provides us with a number of facets which enable us to observe the complex combination of infant and adult elements that may still be present at this age. The fluffy cat which Laura takes with her when leaving home could have some of the meanings of a favourite cuddly toy, but with important new elements. Laura appears to be on the threshold of wishing to look after a living creature, perhaps in preparation for one day becoming a mother, but she is still finding it difficult to take full responsibility for the less attractive and more messy aspects of such a task. This may take rather longer to develop!

There are also two sides to Laura's wish to leave home and be independent. She was full of enthusiasm when she entered the flat-share, but, when confronted with a critical attitude in her flat-mate, she confided to her best friend at work how upset she was and told her how she even felt tempted to go back and live with her parents: "After all, my bedroom at home is still there if I want it." She also realised how much simpler life was when she could rely on her mother doing the housework, shopping and cooking as a regular thing; it wasn't that she could not clean, and in fact did it very well, but it was so infuriating to be expected to do it whenever the cat made a mess.

Laura here is still struggling between her commitment to feeling that she is standing on her own feet and getting on with her career and a younger part of herself that also wants to take it easy and be looked after.

The response of the family

There is a different quality to leaving home in order to take up a place in a hall of residence or to share in a flat from setting up home with a partner. Parents are likely to react to the implications of these different situations in different ways.

When Roy, the motor mechanic, whom we mentioned in the last chapter, told his parents that he was going to move into a bed-sit with his girlfriend, Patsy, they were very taken aback indeed. He knew that this would come as a shock to them since living together before marriage was against their religious beliefs. They had already been disappointed by Roy ceasing to attend church with them after he started work at sixteen. For a time they had turned a blind eye to his having spent nights away from home and accepted without demur accounts of his motor bike having broken down, or even of his needing to stay with a friend and not ride because he had drunk too much. They had hoped to preserve good feelings in the family by avoiding open confrontation. Perhaps Roy's decision would have come as less of a shock had they managed to accept the evidence that their son was spending hours on the phone, talking in a soft voice, and when he went out in the evening left a strong smell of aftershave behind him.

In spite of the more mature aspects of Roy's motivation, it appears that there was still an element of a touchy child in him who strongly resented being told what to do and how to behave. This contributed to his being somewhat hurtful when he and his parents first discussed his leaving home. He protested that he was financially independent and had been able to contribute to the family housekeeping for some time. Although he did not say so to his parents, he and Patsy were in fact talking over how soon they could start a family, and marriage was not far from their minds. Roy perceived himself as being an adult in his own right. He saw his parents' expression of their anxieties just as a deliberate attempt to interfere in his life. We shall return to Roy's fraught relationship with his parents later.

CHAPTER FOUR

CHOOSING FURTHER STUDIES

Decisions of a young person to seek further education may also carry implications for the family. Such decisions may fit in with parental expectations but can also represent a departure from family tradition. We have seen in Roy an example of someone who decided to leave school at sixteen and attend evening classes in technical skills, which was an accepted way forward in his family. A departure from family expectations may prompt different parental reactions. Time and patience may be needed to come to terms with some of the feelings aroused.

Family hopes and disappointments

When Jenny decided to go to business school after having completed her 'A' levels with good grades, her parents were somewhat disappointed, especially as Jenny, on their encouragement, had at first considered some university options. Both parents were teachers in different fields and felt that Jenny would miss out by not having the experience of going to university. The issue of 'family tradition' became particularly evident at the family's Christmas gathering which took place at Jenny's parents' house. Aunt Gladys, her husband – Uncle Jack – and some of their family were there. Two of their children were already at University and there was no question that the younger brother, Alex, would soon follow. The issue of possible choices and the filling out of relevant forms was a major topic of conversation. Aunt Gladys made both Jenny and her parents feel uncomfortable when she remarked on Jenny again being the odd one out in the family. Jenny's parents came to their daughter's rescue by stressing how well she was doing in her business studies, but, later that evening, shared between themselves some measure of disappointment. This had been heightened by Aunt Gladys' remark with its sharp reminder of their break from family tradition. Everyone present at the Christmas gathering either had graduated or was expected to graduate from university, except for their Jenny. It took Jenny's parents some time totally to accept that Jenny's choice had been the right one for her and that she had been right to make it. Jenny was relieved when she eventually felt that her parents understood her need to make her own decision.

Finding one's own path

In some cases finding the most satisfactory path may involve a degree of trial and error. Some young people may find it difficult to make such decisions on their own, and simply follow in their parents' footsteps until their own experiences help them to grow and to find themselves. Jenny knew from the start where she wanted to go and her parents came to accept her decision as being right for her. Mary, a slower developer, initially just conformed to the family pattern and only later became clear about her own inclinations, which her parents then supported.

Mary had taken a year off before going to university. She was spending this time working for an organisation which brought education to children in a third world country. While she was away she wrote to her parents saying that she was beginning to have second thoughts about her choice of subject. She had originally chosen to read English, not because she was particularly interested in it for its own sake, but because her mother had graduated in that subject. For similar reasons she had applied to go to the same college that her mother had attended. Her interests had then shifted in the direction of social and political studies following her experience abroad and her contact with less privileged children which had clearly been unsettling for her. In contrast to Jenny, her decision to go to university followed the norm of the family pattern, and had been somewhat unquestioning. The turmoil occasioned by her being immersed in a wider environment was a spur to her development: her choice of studies acquired a meaning different from following in the family footsteps and going to university largely for its own sake. Instead, it became interwoven not only with her intellectual interests, but also with her emotional experience.

However, Mary's life at university was not easy at first. She had been a rather high achiever at school but now found it difficult to grapple with new, conflicting ideas within a university environment with its philosophical and political arguments. More important than the new intellectual demands however was a powerful emotional challenge due to Mary's much greater awareness of social and political problems arising from her time abroad. She was giving up walking in her mother's footsteps and was trying to find her own path, but this was far from smooth. Although occasionally she felt quite insecure, she also had a feeling from within that she was moving in the direction of becoming her own person. Her parents fortunately were very supportive. They had in fact been slightly worried earlier on when Mary's choice of subject and college totally matched those of her mother, thinking that this might not reflect a real personal choice on their daughter's part, and that she might be fitting into a pre-existing groove.

Changes in direction but keeping family links

Konstantinos' family had lived in the United Kingdom for some time. His parents had both arrived as children and had met in a rather closely knit community in which they both lived. They worked together for many years in the shop they eventually managed to buy. Konstantinos' parents were proud of their achievement, but never made him feel that he would be expected to take on the family business if he did not wish to do so.

Konstantinos enjoyed school and early on showed an interest in science in general, and in medicine in particular. A cousin of his own age suffered from a severe form of a disease which was common in his country of origin. When this cousin's mother took him to the hospital, Konstantinos often went with them. He was only twelve or thirteen when he first said he would like to become a doctor. This project seemed to become confirmed as he grew up and he always felt very much supported in his decision by his parents. Neighbours of Konstantinos, who came from the same country of origin, used to talk a great deal about their son 'the doctor' in a manner which suggested a degree of showing off, but Konstantinos never felt that his parents supported his choice of university studies from a wish to brag about it. Even more important, he did not feel that he would be envied by them if he achieved a better position in life than they had done themselves. By the time he was eighteen and had begun his medical studies, he already knew that he wished to specialise in a branch of medicine which related to the treatment of illnesses such as that from which his cousin suffered. Although Konstantinos went to live in a different town in order to attend university, he always took some favourite food from home with him and frequently returned home for the weekend. His choice of a different educational development from the one of his parents did not by any means sever his links with his culture. He carried his parents' good wishes within him and felt supported by them. A problem between him and his parents did, however, arise later, when it came to his choice of partner, as we shall see later.

Dropping out

Young people may have unexpected difficulties in following their course of studies away from home. In Chapter seven we see how drug abuse nearly wrecked Ann's course. Duncan's predicament confronts us with an example of dropping out on account of early, unresolved, feelings of loss.

Duncan was born in Scotland to very young parents who were both still engaged in their studies. When Duncan was very little, his parents moved to the United States for about three years in order to obtain advanced qualifications. Duncan, the only child at the time, went to live with his maternal grandparents in one of the Scottish islands. His parents were only able to visit very infrequently. On their return his parents did not appear to appreciate how much Duncan had missed them while they were away, nor, on the other hand, how much he missed his grandparents when he returned home to live with them. Two younger sisters were born fairly soon after his parents' return to Scotland. All the children attended schools with high academic standards. Duncan's bewilderment at these major changes in his life did not manifest itself in a waning of his academic ability, which was high. He settled down and became an extremely good achiever in school. His parents were proud of him and, with the support of his teachers, encouraged him to apply for a place at a prestigious university, which he was successful in gaining. He took a year off prior to university, but was much less adventurous than some of his peers; he continued to live at home and worked unostentatiously for a Human Rights organisation in the town where he lived.

At the beginning of the academic year Duncan left to take up his university place with some enthusiasm. It soon, however, became apparent that he had difficulty in living away from home in a hall of residence. He was slightly teased by one of his fellow students when he admitted that he had only ever spent his holidays with his parents. His academic work at university seemed to be of a lower standard than was to be expected from school reports and examination results. Even though the term was only eight weeks long, he returned home for a weekend during his first term. On this occasion he told his parents that he was very unhappy at university, and they were surprised and dismayed that he was not relishing what was felt to be a marvellous opportunity.

On his return home at Christmas time Duncan was somewhat more explicit about how miserable he really felt, but was only able to tell his parents one week before term started that he could not find it in himself to go back. His parents, who admired Duncan's potential and had great faith in his ability, found it extremely difficult to understand how their nineteen-year-old son, who had always done so well in school, could feel anxious about living in a town which was only a six hours train journey away. They felt strongly that he needed support to return to university, and even wrote to his tutor to make sure that a place would be kept for him. During the months Duncan spent at home under some pressure to return to university, he became more and more dispirited. He was also lonely and withdrawn.

It was when the family visited the maternal grandparents at Easter, and they all looked at some photographs of the time Duncan had lived with the grandparents that he broke into tears. It was only then that his parents came to realize how painful both separation from them, and later from the grandparents, had been for him in childhood, and how difficult it was for him to uproot himself again from his current home to go to his university town. For Duncan the difficulty did not lie in the physical distance, but in the very experience of leaving home, with its reminiscence of his earlier departures from home, first his own and then his grandparents. On this occasion the family were able more openly to share their feelings about the meaning of these separations for Duncan in particular. It seemed that this family had developed a culture of achievement and of keeping a 'stiff upper lip' as a way of avoiding painful feelings about separation.

Duncan's parents came to accept that he would drop out for the rest of that academic year, and after that could probably transfer to the university in the town in which they lived. Duncan was extremely relieved about being understood, became much less low in spirits, and also became more sociable. His problem was clearly not an academic one. He did extremely well at the local university. There was no indication whatever of his wishing to drop out from it and he ultimately obtained a first class degree. His parents, who had become more in touch with their own feelings, were more able to understand their son's difficulties in separating and in his reasons for them. They no longer put any pressure on Duncan to leave home during his university years.

Konstantinos's parents had to relinquish any hope they might have entertained about his taking over the shop that they had built up, but could take considerable pride and pleasure in his abilities. Duncan's parents had to relinquish their ambition for their child to attend a prestigious university and to offer supportive understanding for his emotional difficulties which were at least partly related to his experience of early losses.

CHAPTER FIVE

LOVE, SEX AND PARTNERSHIPS

Group life is very important for young people, but as they approach their late teens and early twenties it usually occupies a less central place in their lives. Some young people who have got to know each other in the ups and downs of a group may gradually move out of it, and form more intimate couples. Such relationships at this stage mark a transition between the time when life was spent mostly in a group of friends and a more independent and adult way of life.

Some trial pairings, occasionally still within the group, may take place before a more stable relationship develops. Even if a couple's relationship does not last indefinitely, it may well help each of them to develop their capacity to relate in greater depth.

Nowadays many parents accept that young people may need to experience a number of relationships before they find the right partner. Deeply loving and long-lasting relationships for many young people may not develop until after the age of twenty. Some parents, however, like Roy's mother and father mentioned earlier, believe sex before marriage to be wrong.

Young people will have some kind of picture of their parents in their minds. This may be a loved and admired one, or it may be less loved or even denigrated. Such pictures will influence the image of the kind of partners young people wish to have for themselves. Some parents feel provoked if their child chooses a partner who has a very different approach to life from them. Roy had not wished to provoke his parents by choosing to live with Patsy, but their different views about sex before marriage did complicate family relationships.

Promiscuity

Casual encounters which include a variety of short-lived and superficial sexual experiences are too promiscuous really to be called relationships. Such promiscuity may be an attempt to avoid the pain of the possible failure and loss which can arise in deeper relationships. Such a fear of commitment can sometimes become protracted into later years in life. If parents are able to talk with their children without conveying harsh judgments about their behaviour, and communicate instead their feeling of concern, this may prove very helpful, when promiscuity is seen as a particular problem.

Deepening relationships

Young people of this age are entering adulthood with its possible implications of parenthood. As a couple's relationship becomes more serious, it may provide the ground in which the seeds of a wish to become parents may grow; in other couples this may not necessarily be the case. Difficulty arises and a developing relationship may founder where views on parenthood are not shared even in an early form by both partners.

In her late teens Judith was involved in several not especially intense relationships with boys from a very politically committed group. When she was twenty, however, she fell deeply in love with a fellow sociology student, Daniel, and really felt committed to him. One weekend, when her parents were visiting her at University, she asked them whether they minded if she brought Daniel along for lunch. Her parents were pleased, but took care not to ask any embarrassing questions or appear to have expectations of the relationship being firmly established. Judith and Daniel spent a summer vacation travelling together in Europe and visited some of Daniel's family who lived in France. Both young people clearly felt comfortable enough about their relationship to introduce their partner to their family. After a year or more in a steady partnership, Judith had become progressively involved. She was thinking about setting up home with Daniel on a long term basis. Such a commitment was frightening for Daniel, who then decided to apply for an extension of his studies abroad, and gave clear indications that he wished to disengage himself from the relationship with

Judith. Judith was devastated. She spoke with her friends, but also, in tears, phoned her mother, who encouraged her to come home for a few days. This she did.

Judith's mother had clearly tuned in to the perception that her twenty-year-old daughter needed at this point to be cared for as a much younger girl. Judith in turn was very appreciative of the way that her parents looked after her. The experience of actually being cared for with attentive, but not intrusive concern, helped to restore a feeling of having something good and benevolent within herself; literally she was helped to feel more 'together', while she had earlier felt in disarray, as if in pieces.

Judith and Daniel's relationship had seemed to evolve naturally into making love together. In its literal sense 'love making' is closely related to increasing the amount of love that can be lavished on others, and for Judith this extended into thoughts of family life, but Daniel did not share Judith's wish for such commitment.

Roy was popular with girls and had experienced several sexual encounters before he met Patsy. Although he found his parents' religious beliefs too strict, and had already stopped going to church, family values were important to him. His wish to set up home with Patsy was based on a firm commitment to the relationship, which was very likely eventually to lead to marriage – needless to say to the pleasure of his family. While the idea of a baby proved too formidable for Daniel, Roy and Patsy spent much of their time talking about when they would start a family and they were both delighted, when, shortly after setting up home together, Patsy became pregnant.

Homosexuality and prejudice

In earlier teenage years attraction between people of the same sex is very frequent and forms part of getting to know masculine and feminine aspects of one's own personality. A more confident knowledge of one's sexual orientation has generally been reached by the 18 to 20 year age group. Many of the anxieties experienced by gay or lesbian young people are related to the discrimination and general homophobia which they may encounter in the heterosexual community.

Although Roy had shocked his parents by his intention to set up home with a girl before marriage, and disappointed them by not continuing to share their religious beliefs, he was, nevertheless, not immune from prejudice and could be shocked himself. He had very firm beliefs about sexual identity. When John, one of Roy's old school friends, who worked in a different part of the country, came to visit him and Patsy in their new flat, he told the couple that he had also set up home, and mentioned that his partner was a young man. He told them that he had 'come out' since he had last seen Roy, and that his parents, with some struggle, had been able to accept his gay identity. Roy was very shocked, and John was very hurt at seeing this. Although he managed not to say much, his feelings were very apparent from his expression. Patsy noticed that Roy had not taken the opportunity, as planned, of asking John to be best man at their wedding.

Patsy and Roy discussed the matter after John had left. Patsy had no reservations about John on account of his homosexuality. She was very taken aback when she heard how adamant Roy was about not being able to face the possibility of a gay best man. A heated argument developed between them. Patsy tried to make Roy change his mind by reminding him that he had told her that John would make a very nice speech at the wedding, because he was very articulate and would tell all sorts of funny stories and recount childhood memories. This argument did not go down well with Roy, who retorted that he could easily find a better best man. Patsy then added, with a touch of irony, that perhaps Roy was worried that John might recount too many childhood memories. She was referring to reminiscences Roy had shared with her of his first years in secondary school when he had been involved, like so many boys of that age, in various forms of sexual play and exploration with male school friends, including John.

Patsy, in spite of feeling resentful on John's behalf, was able to jog Roy's memory and feelings with sufficient humour for him not to feel got at. Roy became able to think in a less judgmental way both about John and his own earlier homosexual experiences. It is to Patsy's credit that John was eventually asked to be best man at the wedding.

Returning to John's comments about his parents

having adjusted to his 'coming out' with a struggle: an important factor was that John happened to be an only child and his parents may perhaps have regretted that they were not going to become grandparents. This, rather than homophobia, seemed to lie at the root of their struggle.

CHAPTER SIX

DIFFERENT USES OF LEISURE

Leisure implies time of one's own to choose any activity, or even none at all. Young people give this freedom very different interpretations. For most of them, whether working or studying, there is a natural divide between the activities of the week and those of the week-end. Part of the tragedy associated with unemployment is that no such natural divide occurs.

In the course of this book we often refer to the different paths followed by young people in their search to develop a clear identity. We now look at the shape this search takes in the use of leisure time. Very broadly there are two ends of the spectrum which divide the use of such free time; those activities which further integration in the personality and those which disrupt what integration is already there. We discuss the second type of activity in the next chapter. In this chapter we see how leisure activities can bring about some important developmental processes, such as the waning of envy and the waxing of admiration.

The use of leisure as a means of change and development

Tony's father is a great maker and mender of all sorts of things. He carries out numerous repairs in the house and has cabinet-making as a hobby. Tony had been quite a rebellious adolescent in his middle teens and often fairly scornful about his father's activities: "What a way to spend your weekends, Dad," he used to say. "Why try to repair the surface of that old coffee table, instead of buying a new one? We're not that broke." He even gave some quasi-fatherly advice to his father, suggesting that there were better things to do than mending jobs around the house. "Wouldn't mum like to go out for a week-end to the seaside?" In this rather grandiose mood, he seemed to have overlooked the fact that his mother had no particular liking for coastal resorts, and that she generally appreciated her husband's skill and the pleasure it gave him. But Tony was obviously convinced at the time that he would make a better husband than his father.

A very gradual change took place in Tony. A small episode illustrates the shift of perspective in his view of his father's talents. One evening, when Tony's girlfriend, Maureen, came round, it emerged in conversation that the catch on her necklace – which had belonged to her grandmother – had broken and, being antique, might be both difficult and expensive to repair commercially. Tony's father said that he might be able to help and in fact, by experimenting with his tools, managed to restore the spring in the broken catch.

In the patronising advice Tony used to give to his father about how to be a better man and a better husband, one can perhaps sense, not just rivalry, but also an element of envy. It was difficult for the younger Tony to accept that his father had skills which he did not himself possess. This resentful feeling tied him up in knots, and made it difficult for him to develop such skills himself. Such development only becomes possible when feelings of admiration begin to predominate over those of envy. Tony really experienced admiration for his father when he mended the catch of Maureen's necklace. Soon after this, something went wrong with Tony's stereo. Instead of automatically taking it to a shop for repair, he was surprised to hear himself actually asking his father if he could teach him how to repair it. He discovered that he himself could be quite skilled in this area of making and mending. When he was younger, he had played the drums in a band of friends. The way he practised at home often tested the patience of his parents to the limit. It seemed at times that he enjoyed the provocation of making a very loud noise more than the pleasure of making music. He had remained on the fringe of the band, but as his friends got to know of his making and mending talent, he was often asked to help with technical hiccups in the equipment and he became more involved in the musical activity of the group. What started as a kind of pottering with wires and loudspeakers became a further enjoyable use of his leisure time.

Tony seems in a sense to have entered into a process of identification with his father's capacity to enjoy repairing. He could now take in admired qualities rather than denigrating them; admiration had prevailed over envy. This was the beginning of a benign developmental process. As well as influencing his feeling of who he was, his capacity for enjoyment of his leisure was increased. He had also become less of a rebellious adolescent and more of an adult.

Leisure on wheels

The move from a pushbike in early teens to a motorbike, or even to a car, can be a big influence on spare time for many young people. Roy had saved to buy his motorbike from the time he left school. Some of his car mending took place outside people's own houses, and he thus needed his bike for work as well as using it for leisure. For many young people the possession of a car or motorbike is invested with a meaning of potency and can be seen as a status symbol. This may be of special significance for any young person acquiring such a vehicle for the first time, as it was for some of Roy's acquaintances. However, although the day that Roy bought his motorbike was undoubtedly an important one for him, he did not seem to need it as an external support to buoy up his feeling of confidence in his own masculinity.

Matters were different as far as Luke was concerned. He started to borrow his older brother's motor bike as soon as he was legally allowed to ride it, or even a little earlier. It was only with such external support, full of power, that he felt he had sufficient confidence in his own drive. It was, in fact, only after he became the very proud possessor of a motor bike himself, that he was able to ask a girl to go out with him. When nineteen, he used to go quite regularly to the pub, where he played pool and often chatted to the barmaid, Gloria, who was young, attractive and very sought after by his friends and himself. She knew that he had a motor bike, and told him, in a rather provocative tone, that he could pick her up after closing time when he got himself a car, as she did not like to wear a helmet and freeze. Luke took this joke quite seriously and asked his father – at first quite politely – if he could borrow the car on Saturday night. His father said firmly that the car was not insured for him to drive, and that he would have to make do with his motor bike. Luke became very angry and abusive and said that he would give his father the money for adding his name to the insurance – this only needed a telephone call and his father could do it straight away. He added that his father and mother never went out – which was not in general true. What got under Luke's father's skin, and made him lose his temper, was the implicit message in Luke's words that he had a right to priority over his parents to go out and enjoy himself on a Saturday night. It is not infrequent for young people in their teens to put across to their parents the message that they have cornered the market in sexuality: the parents are past it and must make room for them. It can be very difficult to try to understand and bear this provocation rather than react to it in a punitive way.

There is a risk that a row of the kind Luke had with his father may escalate and finally leave such resentment on both sides that no return to normal relationships seems possible. A young person may then leave home, slamming the door with very bitter feelings. Yielding by the parents to the pressure coming from the younger generation in order to avoid conflict and confrontation does not provide a solution. On the other hand, finding enough distance in order not to respond aggressively in spite of feeling provoked, may, in the heat of the moment, be far from easy. Parents may have to struggle to maintain a conviction, firstly within themselves, but also with their son or daughter, that leisure and enjoyment are needed by both generations, rather than being exclusive to only one of them.

Luke's compulsive pressure for use of the car before he could find expression for his masculinity, speaks of a real lack of self esteem. Unlike Tony, he has not been able to take inside himself an admired picture of his father, but is still caught up in a very competitive relationship with him. This suggests that he can only enjoy himself on vicarious power in contrast with Tony's ability to learn from a father he admires.

Leisure interests as part of the building of identity

Alison was eighteen. She had, from infancy been taken up hill and down dale by her mountain loving parents and, together with her brother and sister, had enjoyed the experience. In these outings the family often found interesting ways of reaching their destination, without always sticking to paths to be found on the map. Alison developed an interest in nature and took botany as one of her 'A' level exams. She also joined a walking club in her teens. Although she felt strongly that she very much enjoyed her leisure time and derived great pleasure from contact with nature, there was a quivering doubt in her mind which at times spoiled such enjoyment: in doing this am I just literally following in my parents' footsteps? In the process of trying to find out whether she really had it in herself to devote so much of her free time to this kind of activity, she felt she had to challenge herself and join a mountaineering club. Together with her boyfriend, she took part in weekend climbs in Scotland and Wales, which, by their nature, involved a degree of danger.

This somewhat dare-devil period, which fairly soon abated, was very much related to testing out whether such activity felt intrinsically genuine to her, and to a need to understand for herself that it was not simply a form of imitation of her parents' interests, or, on the other hand, a rivalrous attempt to surpass their achievements. By the time she was nearly twenty she appeared to have worked through these doubts which had led her to a period of strenuous and dangerous activity. Love for nature, together with an adventurous spirit, came to be part of her character. Her interests in nature blended with her wider interests; she liked, for instance, to take part in sponsored walks for environmental causes.

CHAPTER SEVEN

CAUSES FOR CONCERN: ANTI-SOCIAL ACTIVITIES

The period of transition from childhood to adulthood is unlikely to follow a straight path or to progress evenly. In so far as this is a time for the development of what may gradually become personal standards, it may well include periods of considerable confusion about right and wrong. In the early and middle teens many young people may have been experimenting to some extent with drugs, drink and rebelliousness or minor delinquency. Although, as we said earlier, there is a general tendency for young people aged between eighteen and twenty to become less involved in group activities, this does not always happen. A group may stay together and turn into an anti-social gang, or young people may build up the type of companionship or alliances which lead them on a dangerous path.

In this chapter we think about young people whose activities carry potentially very serious consequences. Fortunately not all adolescents confront their parents with this high degree of anxiety. When Luke asked his father for use of the precious car that would enable him to take Gloria out, he conveyed the feeling that he had a right to something like temporary ownership of it. Although he was rather arrogant and unpleasant, he was at least asking to use the family car, not stealing it. A very different state of mind brings about the 'joy riding' or illicit taking and driving away of cars, which are subsequently abandoned, sometimes in a damaged state, and on occasion leading to more serious consequences. Young people may get a 'high' from what they experience as a sense of adult potency, which, of course, is stolen, and not actually their own. Such 'joyriding' can so often bring about a great deal of sorrow. Many of these instances of taking and driving away occur at the hands of younger teenagers, but can still continue into the late teens.

Delinquent behaviour and debilitating environments

Gary was the fourth boy in his family. When he was two years old a fifth child was born. His mother was depressed after the birth, and not very available to Gary. Gary developed a grievance towards both parents that did not, unfortunately, become less bitter over the years. The lack of a trusting relationship with his parents made it difficult for him to form helpful relationships with his teachers. Gary's involvement in delinquency did not start with stealing cars. He seemed to be attracted by anything that defied authority, such as smoking in the school toilets when he was eleven years old. In order first of all to buy cigarettes and later drugs, he often took money from his mother's wallet or stole from his older brothers, some of whom were working. Unfortunately there was not enough communication between Gary's family or his school for the warning signals to be sufficiently noticed so that Gary could be helped out of a downward spiral.

By the time Gary had left school he was living in a world of delinquency, and had gradually shifted from smoking dope to experimenting with hard drugs. When he was eighteen, he and a fellow member of his gang were caught trying to take and drive away a car. A talented probation officer, sensitive to Gary's predicament and feeling of emotional isolation, managed to make contact with him and get through to the problems of his use and abuse of hard drugs. The probation officer knew that he could not help Gary with the problem of stealing until he had overcome his addictive trends and was successful in getting him to seek treatment and in getting his referral accepted by a centre for drug addiction.

The attraction of drugs and drink: a false solution

Finding out for oneself what to consider is right or wrong, especially when no longer, as in childhood, accepting parents' standards as a package deal, is part of the process of growing up. It links with the attempt to consolidate a sense of identity. This can be a painful process and drink and drugs can be used as a way to obliterate difficulties rather than attend to them with a degree of thought. Drugs may offer not only temporary relief from anxiety and conflict but also provide temporary pleasure. Soft drugs, such as cannabis, may have an effect which has something in common with the intoxicating effects of alcohol. Becoming intoxicated with drink or becoming 'stoned' with such drugs may be experienced as pleasurable for as long as it lasts, but prolonged and compulsive use inhibits development.

The deleterious effects of some drugs such as L.S.D. and heroin are well known. At times young people may not be aware of just how dangerous L.S.D. can be. A bad 'trip' can lead to very frightening feelings of disintegration and of going mad. Professional help may be needed to help to overcome addictive usage, as was the case with Gary, and, as we shall see, with Ann.

Group pressure, as in other antisocial activities, may play a significant part in encouraging the evasion of the difficult process of really establishing one's own identity.

The abuse of drugs can form part of some students' way of life. It is sometimes part of a university ritual to celebrate the end of a period of study – especially after swotting for an examination – with the type of leisure that could, in its extreme, be described as 'mind-blowing'.

Ann went to university and spent much of her time with a group which was heavily into both drink and drugs. With her friends, on many week-ends, but especially after examinations, she used to merge day and night, carrying on from one hangover to the next drink, together with liberal use of what are sometimes called 'party going drugs', such as Speed and Ecstasy. This often took place at gatherings where the aim was to get high, forget hard work, and take a holiday not only from actual working, but also from thinking itself.

Ann did not often go home for the weekend, although the university she attended was fairly near her home town, but in talking with her parents on the phone she sometimes referred to going away from college for the weekend with different boys. This, understandably, worried her parents considerably. Ann did not take kindly to their clear expression of disapproval, and, for a time, rarely went home during the vacation either. Ann's behaviour is rather extreme. She kept herself constantly on the go. Behind her flight into casual sexual relationships and experimentation with drugs, lay her difficulty in thinking over and coming to terms with conflicting feelings about the kind of person she wanted to be and the way that she wanted to lead her life. She functioned somewhat precariously in her studies, but felt progressively unstable, and even thought of dropping out. The idea of abandoning university life seemed to be part of an attack on her parents and parental values. She in fact came to feel increasingly miserable because in her heart of hearts she sensed that she had in some way smashed up a good relationship with her parents. Altogether she felt very anxious and confused. She was caught up in a vicious circle as a consequence of her reliance on drink and drugs, which obviously only gave her temporary relief. When thinking of dropping out, she spoke to her personal tutor, who strongly advised her to seek help from the university counsellor.

Ann's conflicts related to her difficulty in grappling with finding herself and her own values, and it was helpful for her to talk with somebody who was totally outside both her family circle and friends in her own age group. Work with the university counsellor helped Ann to begin to think about the upheaval she was facing in the transition to becoming her own person. The experience of being understood, in contrast to that of feeling suspended in mid-air, helped to lessen her sense of lacking any sort of direction. She became interested in getting to know herself and made good use of the help offered.

Ann's experience of counselling provided her with some help in thinking about her conflicts, and her frantic way of life quietened down as a consequence. Her relationship with her parents also improved. Ann started going out more steadily with a young man with whom she shared some interests as well as a mutual physical attraction and the quality of the relationship seemed to be much deeper than any previous one. Ann had been living in a kind of no man's land, not yet having found her own frame of reference, but clearly having rejected that of her parents.

CHAPTER EIGHT

EATING DISORDERS AND DEPRESSION

Eating disorders

Young people are often preoccupied with appearance and the way their bodies work, particularly from the time when sexual development begins to take place and their appearance undergoes important changes. Many more girls than boys suffer from eating disorders. A fiercely dieting eighteen-year-old girl may have had worries when her periods started and the shape of her body began to change. For instance, a girl in her early teens said, 'my body has taken over in spite of myself'. It is not accidental that very severe weight loss due to refusal of food also brings about the cessation of periods. Such an occurrence has an undeniable physiological cause, but is also meaningful in terms of a rejection of the self as a growing sexual being. Eating disorders, especially when very serious, raise great anxieties including the risk of death. It may be necessary to seek medical and other professional help. The symptom itself is the outcome of deep and very severe anxieties in the adolescents concerned which may even spread infectious ripples among their contemporaries. Some of this anxiety, however, may be carried by parents, relatives, friends and sometimes therapists, more than is apparently carried by the adolescent herself.

An internal problem with external repercussions

Barbara is eighteen and in the final year of her 'A' level course. She was a difficult feeder as a baby. Her little brother was born when she was three years old, and, at this time, she developed a large number of food fads. She started refusing foods she had previously liked, and, for about a year, would only eat food which had been pureed.

Barbara's parents separated around the time when she started school. She lived with her mother, but saw her father frequently. She was still a difficult feeder when she reached puberty, and this changed into a nearly complete rejection of food between the ages of twelve and thirteen. It was only after she had recovered from this first bout of anorexia that her periods started. As well as being a good all-round achiever in school, she was also interested in cookery, and loved to prepare meals, although herself only eating small portions.

During the second term of this second year in the sixth

form, her anorectic symptoms returned in a very marked way. She completely stopped having meals with the family. She became very keen on balancing a very small food intake with quite intensive exercise, so that no weight gain should occur. In fact considerable weight loss followed. The main worry about this seemed to be carried by her parents, while Barbara was mainly preoccupied with being too fat. Barbara's English teacher, who was also the head of the sixth form, was particularly worried by the alarming preoccupation with weight, food and body image spreading within Barbara's form. The process seemed to have been initiated by a girl called Nancy, who had herself been extremely thin, but who now had put weight back on again, as the preoccupation with food and weight spread among her classmates. Some members of the form were considerably more susceptible than others to experiencing this kind of anxiety.

Barbara's parents, despite their divorce, continued to share concern about their children. When the sixth form put on a Shakespeare play as part of their preparation for the English 'A' level examination, Barbara's mother and father both attended and had an opportunity to talk with parents of other obsessive dieters, and shared some of their worries with them. They had not realised until then that there seemed to be a small epidemic of anorexia in the sixth form. One particular couple to whom Barbara's parents talked, mentioned the very helpful understanding they had received from their doctor, following which their daughter had started psychotherapy. As Barbara's weight had now gone down to rather alarming levels, her parents decided to follow the same procedure and spoke with their doctor. Barbara, at first, was not keen to begin therapy, pleading a need to use all available time to study. She was, however, gradually persuaded to accept a few exploratory interviews, and eventually engaged in psychotherapy which helped her to realise and come to terms with her underlying anxieties.

The impact of traumatic external circumstances

Marcus, aged twenty, had come to London as a refugee from his much tormented country. He had come with his mother, but had lost his father and brother in tragic circumstances in a civil war. There had been considerable food shortages in the country he came from, and when he arrived in the United Kingdom he was very underweight. He started eating a huge quantity of easily accessible food, such as cereal, biscuits and chocolate. He and his mother had been brought over together with a number of other refugees. Very fortunately a group for victims of disasters was organised locally in an attempt to relate to their traumatic experience. At one of the group meetings where the issue of how the young people could deal with unbearable memories was discussed, Maria said in a very flat voice, "I have a very good way to cope with it – I just binge and then make myself sick." A very angry and outspoken nineteen-year-old snapped back saying "Everybody knows only girls put their head down the lavatory." Marcus who was sitting next to Maria, and had looked at her with interest and surprise when she had spoken about her symptoms, gathered the courage needed to say that he himself had been bingeing and making himself sick since he had left his country. This comment was almost silenced by an assertion from another girl who found it practically impossible to stop and really reflect on their experiences. She seemed to want to put an end to this discussion by focusing only on the bingeing and ignoring the vomiting, by saying "Sure, we all eat a lot when we arrive in a place where there is food; we have been starving for months in our country."

The matter could have been allowed to rest at this point, but the group leader was able to help the young people to think about how the symptoms described by Marcus and Maria, could be connected with their traumatic experiences. The voracious bingeing seemed to fulfil the function of smothering feelings of anxiety, emptiness and loss. The vomiting, on the other hand, seemed to be related, at least partly, to the fact that both these young people had had literally indigestible experiences thrust upon them, and being sick could represent a very concrete way of getting rid of them; in other words a state of mind became transformed into a state of body.

These latter examples refer to external experiences; eating disorders, however, may occur purely in response to internal conflicts as in the case of Barbara. Quite frequently a combination of internal and external factors contribute to the development of such problems. A bulimic illness, expressed by bingeing and vomiting, is not usually associated with such traumatic circumstances as those referred to above. Nevertheless such symptoms are quite frequently associated with a series of conflicts or anxieties which have not been emotionally digested.

Depression: undermining external factors

A variety of meanings may underlie the descriptive symptoms of what is referred to as depression. It is characterised by a listless approach to life, which includes a general lack of initiative and vitality. There may be a general predominance of external or internal factors, or a fair amount of both, in the background.

Alan, aged nineteen, left school with very poor examination results but had not in any case intended to use these as a springboard to any form of continuing education. He was not successful in getting a place in a training scheme, nor could he find any employment. He generally got up very late, although his mother did try to get him down to have breakfast with the family. He spent a great deal of his time watching television, mainly sport, and occasionally read the paper if one was lying around. He spent a lot of his social security money on cigarettes. His father, who had been a miner, had recently been made redundant and together with an ex-colleague, had, with a mixture of considerable skill and good fortune, managed to set up a small business which had some call for manual labour. His father, with some difficulty, managed to get Alan to help him, as Alan himself had become very lethargic. Alan needed both some change in the external circumstances, together with some warm and firm encouragement from his father, to emerge from his depression and lack of vitality. He was very socially isolated. The fact that his older brother was married and lived away from home contributed to this. As with Beverley, in Chapter 2, emerging from unemployment was a saving grace. Once he started earning, he found it easier to go out in the evening to meet other young people. In time, he acquired a girlfriend, which helped to alleviate his depressed feelings of being unlikeable. By the time he was twenty, life had brightened up for him a great deal. In Alan's case, external factors were important, not only in the cause, but in the resolution of his state of mind. We now want to give an example of a different type of depression which seems to be more associated with internal feelings of bitterness and grievance.

Depression: internal factors

Eva was nineteen and had come as an au pair to a small town in England to stay with Michael and Julia Smith and their three children. The Smith family was a friendly and easy-going one. Michael worked locally as the owner of a video rental shop and Julia had a small mail order business in children's clothes which she designed and made herself. The Smiths were struck by a sullen quality in Eva which they initially attributed to homesickness. This proved, however, not to be the case, because when she started talking about her home town and her family, she seemed to have nothing to say that was not critical. Julia, who was very sensitive, got the feeling that this continual, ruminatory criticism might contribute to a kind of worn out quality in Eva, who always appeared to be lacking in energy, found it difficult to get out of bed, and seemed to have to make a tremendous effort to undertake apparently undemanding tasks. When asked to help at breakfast and get the children ready for school, which Julia had taken to be part of Eva's task, Eva complained. She said that the specific times she was to work had not been stated in their agreement, but that she would fulfil her obligations during the day.

It was clear that Eva lacked energy and vitality and seemed caught up in a spiral of complaints that used up what little energy she had. Something came across from her, which seemed to suggest that she was entitled to be depressed, and would not be deprived of that right. Only three weeks after Eva's arrival, Julia found a paper advertising posts for au pairs, left ostentatiously by Eva on the coffee table. Julia decided to bring into the open what had become apparent, namely that Eva was not happy in their household. Eva reluctantly admitted that she had been making enquiries about a job in London, and that she hated living in a small provincial town. She also seemed to be looking for an unlikely job where there would be very little housework, and at most one child in the family, because she did not really like working with children. As you might imagine, Eva did move out, leaving behind a trail of bitterness, including an unhappy experience for the children in the family.

When someone is very full of grievances it may sometimes be associated with experiences of deprivation or even of abuse. Eva's behaviour could be thought of as depressed in that she could not partake actively in work, and was morose in character. She differed from Alan in that the origin of this feeling seemed to be mainly internal, rather than based in any particularly undesirable external experiences. Eva's reluctance to be helpful with the Smith's children might be very directly related to a perception of them as the equivalent of younger brothers and sisters. There is no doubt that she resented the fact that her parents had had several children after her, but it is quite usual, in normally supportive family circumstances, to be able to modify feelings of jealousy as part of the process of growing up. Eva's parents, as we shall see in the next chapter, did appear to be able to think about the needs of all their children and to be sensitive to their feelings. Eva's resentment, however, extended outside the family, as she had developed a very jaundiced outlook on life, which she seemed to want to, or even need to, hold on to. Such clinging to her grievances made it very difficult to help her; the Smiths were clearly well-intentioned. Eva at that time was particularly entrenched in her attitude.

Some young people, even if they have a chip on their shoulder, may be less impervious than Eva was, when confronted with good experiences arising in late adolescence. This kind of 'second chance', as offered by the benevolent Smith family, might help to modify negative feelings about parents. Even in Eva's case, as we shall see later, some opening may have been made for better relations later on with parent-type figures.

Depression: bearing sadness and loss; isolation; fears of suicide

Depression can also be a consequence of loss in the external world, accompanied by a related sense of sadness.

Cecily, whom we discuss more fully in chapter nine, lost her mother in a car accident when she was eighteen. Following this, she became less outgoing as she experienced her feelings relating to this sudden death of her mother. These included her deep sadness, but also feelings of rage and unfairness about the accident. Such loss needs to be recognized and mourned, and help or support may be needed. In earlier chapters we described how Judith was comforted in bearing the loss of her relationship with Daniel by her parents. Duncan's repeated loss of contact with those he loved was largely unrecognized by himself or his family until after he left home to go to university. Those suffering an experience of sudden and violent death and loss of their homeland, as in the case of the refugees described earlier in this chapter may, as we shall see, need help before they can bear to accept the real depth of their feelings.

It is often extremely painful to bear the sadness of loss, as Cecily did, but there is usually some hope of coming to terms with it eventually. However, some young people may not be able to relate to their sadness in such a way that they can eventually overcome it on their own. They may become very low in spirits, possibly isolate themselves and lack a sense of meaning in life, at times to the extent of having thoughts of suicide. In addition to parental care, professional help is then needed.

CHAPTER NINE

A NEW STAGE OF LIFE BEGINS

The impact of separation on family members

As we said in the introduction, when young people embark on the journey which leads to final separation from the parental home, a time of upheaval not only for the children, but also for the parents, follows. Looking back, no-one can feel that the upbringing of their children has been as good as they would have wished. Parents may have to find forgiveness both for their children and for themselves for mistakes that have been made. Parents may also have to adjust to returning to living alone, or as a couple, in what may feel like an empty nest.

This watershed in normal development, which parents must have originally experienced for themselves when they were adolescents, is bound to have an element of pain which may be felt to a greater degree by either the parents or the children at different times. It is frequently the parents who bear the brunt more directly. The young person is moving on to a new stage in life; for him or her the parting can represent an opening, while many parents, especially when the last child leaves home, have to relate to a feeling of absence. Konstantinos's mother, although very proud of her son's place in medical school, felt sad and low when he left and was very glad when he came home, and also took some of her home-cooked food back to university with him. Laura's parents thought her move into a flat share was a constructive one for her. Her mother in particular felt that it would do Laura some good to be directly confronted with some of the responsibilities of housekeeping. Laura, however, was the last child to leave home, and the parents not only missed ongoing family life, but were even surprised at missing the frequent ringing of the telephone which they had in the past found so irritating. They did, though, decide to go together to evening classes to learn Italian in preparation for a coming holiday, and in this way, were pleased to have more time to take up some of their old hobbies.

The departures from home of both Konstantinos and Laura had been discussed in the family, were seen as a natural development, and did not come as a surprise. When the move out of the parental home is likely to create conflict, as it did in Roy's case, the decision to leave may be taken quite abruptly, leaving a sharper kind of pain behind. As we shall see in this chapter, that particular jagged edge was, however, able to be repaired.

Sometimes a child, such as Duncan, may be carrying a great deal of the emotion connected with separation on behalf of the family, to the detriment of his development. In his case this was eventually addressed at a later point in life, although it had its roots in early childhood. Some departures, such as that of Harry, who ended up homeless in London, must, sadly, leave very unhappy and unresolved feelings behind.

Going and coming back

Sometimes more or less grown up children may put across a very clear message of having itchy feet and being all ready to go, longing for total independence; parents, understandably, can take this at face value. Some young people may need to go through a phase of homesickness, or occasionally even return home for a time before developing a real capacity to stand on their own two feet.

When Eva, whom we referred to in the previous chapter, decided to visit her parents for Christmas, a problematic situation arose. She had left home saying quite firmly that she was going to earn her living abroad working as an au pair, adding that she was most unlikely to be coming back for holidays. At that time she had seemed quite prepared for the role of looking after other people's children, even with a degree of enthusiasm, which, as we saw, soon waned.

When Eva was at home, her four younger brothers had shared two rooms from early childhood. Eva, being a girl, as well as being the eldest, had the privilege of a room of her own. When she left, her parents decided that Ingmar, the eldest of her brothers, who at the time was preparing for school leaving examinations, should be given an opportunity of having his own room, as he often studied until late at night.

Eva's parents were surprised, but very pleased indeed to hear that Eva would, after all, come home for Christmas. They realised that she might be upset at no longer having her own room so they wrote to her about the shift in the sleeping arrangements. The parents talked over whether it would be appropriate to move Ingmar back to sharing with his brother, but felt it would not be right as far as he was concerned. They also thought that Eva would not feel happy in her old room now that it was full of her brother's posters and belongings. Eva therefore slept on the studio couch in the living room, as visitors to the family normally did. This highlighted her feeling of being, by then, just a visitor. Eva put on a brave face, but was in fact so hurt and resentful that she was unable to talk about it with her parents, although this might have helped her to understand their point of view. She was, however, able to confide her perception of being thrown out of the family to her Aunt Ingrid, her father's younger sister, with whom she had always had a good relationship. Their discussion helped her not only to feel understood, but also to understand something of her parents' side of the problem. She was even able to reflect with her aunt on her tendency to hold on to grievances. Aunt Ingrid, at a tactful moment, was able to tell Eva that she herself had been very pleased to move into her brother's – that is Eva's father's – room when he had left home!

Conflicting points of view

The above example illustrates how circumstances can lead to feelings of rejection being acutely experienced by a young person. It is also not infrequent for parents to feel themselves rejected.

When Roy told his mother and father that he was going to set up home with Patsy without getting married, they experienced this as an utter rejection of the values which they felt very strongly about, and had taken for granted that Roy would also uphold. They had earlier turned a blind eye to the fact that Roy's sexual life was clearly departing from their very firmly held principles. Roy's offended attitude, along with the rather rigid approach of his parents, caused an ongoing rift in the family for some time. His parents found his dismissive attitude towards their standards extremely hard to bear. They were also very hurt by his treatment of them as bigoted and narrow-minded; it was, for them, as if they had given him nothing good. Roy really believed that what he was doing was perfectly acceptable, and felt his parents to be unreasonable. He found it difficult to say he was sorry and his parents also could not bring themselves to forgive him. For some time Roy and his girlfriend, Patsy, did not join in the longstanding family tradition of a shared Sunday lunch. Roy's older brothers and sisters had adhered in a fairly conventional way to the family's standards, so that Roy's behaviour was experienced as a totally unexpected and wounding bolt from the blue by his parents.

Parents may indeed have a variety of experiences with their children during their teenage years. We can observe different qualities in the previous two examples. Eva was hurt because she no longer felt treated as a child of the family, Roy's parents felt hurt because they saw their son as having rejected their parental standards.

Painful issues for parents

Parents may at times have objections regarding their children's friends, partners or way of life. By the time their children have reached this age, they will, however, be aware that being authoritarian or expressing their opinion in a highly judgemental way, may be very counterproductive.

Ann's parents, although perhaps a little rigid, were very caring of her and found the breakdown of their previous friendly contact with their daughter extremely troubling. Ann did not seem to be very welcoming of their visits to the university town where she studied. She made it clear that what she saw as a monthly ritual of a shared dinner was not her idea of fun. On the discovery of what Ann's idea of fun really was, her parents were dismayed. The very strong smell of incense in her room and the presence of rather dazed looking young people on different visits made it clear to them that there was a liberal consumption of cannabis there, and that this might have been one of the reasons why their very generous allowance to Ann never seemed to be enough.

They came to realize that their daughter had willingly

become kidnapped by a group of fellow students which seemed to possess many of the characteristics of an anti-parental gang. They were deeply worried that they might lose Ann both to the gang and to addiction to drugs, alcohol and promiscuity. They were, fortunately, able to give one another a great deal of mutual support, so that they were not completely overwhelmed but were able to respond constructively. Although they found a way of conveying to Ann that they were clearly in the picture about what was happening, they could maintain a degree of closeness to her which enabled Ann to feel neither excessively intruded upon, nor given up for lost. Her parents were extremely relieved when Ann told them that she had approached the university counsellor.

Ann's parents did not approve of their daughter's choice of friends or of their lifestyle, but realized that continuous criticism could only represent an added incentive for their daughter's allegiance to the values of this particular gang.

At times similar feelings of disagreement with a son's or daughter's choices might refer to that of a partner rather than to that of a group of friends.

We described earlier the very satisfactory relationship between Konstantinos and his parents. This was severely tested when Konstantinos fell in love with a fellow medical student, a beautiful Irish girl, Kitty. When he was disinclined to join the family business his parents had in no way pressurrised him to do so. However, it was a great deal more difficult for both of them, his mother in particular, to accept that he would not marry 'a nice girl' in a church of their own religion. They could not imagine having grandchildren who were not entirely part of their culture. When Konstantinos told his parents that his relationship with Kitty was serious, and that one day they might get married, his mother could not help bursting into tears. Konstantinos did not waver in his decision, but was sensitive to his mother's feelings and realized that although he had a right to choose, his choice had come as a painful surprise to his parents.

Parental and professional help

We have already seen a number of examples of how parents have responded to their children in a helpful way in this book. Parents can often help their eighteen to twenty year old children simply by standing by and offering thoughtful attention to their feelings. This may be at the level of thinking about future developments of any kind in their lives and sharing thoughts with them when it feels appropriate. It can also be helpful to be able to tolerate disagreement about future plans as in the case of Jenny, or disappointment about a choice of partner, as in the case of Konstantinos.

At times it may feel right to welcome a child home at a moment of crisis: Judith's parents realized, after her relationship with Daniel broke up, that their daughter needed to be at home and treated for a time as a younger child. The fact that her parents could bear her misery, and think about it without being worn down, helped Judith to feel that she was again more lovable herself. Eva's parents were able to give careful attention to her feelings when she returned home, but did not allow family life to be disrupted.

Parents, as we saw with Ann, may need to convey their feelings of disagreement with their child's way of life, but nevertheless seek to maintain, at times with great effort, a friendly and supportive relationship. This support provides solid ground to stand on at a time of great emotional upheaval. It may be possible, as we saw with Barbara, even for separated parents to support each other and their child in times of need.

Sometimes parents may, on account of their own difficulties, be unable to respond to their children's problems directly. In some instances, whatever care is provided by parents, the degree of distress may call for outside help, as with Ann, Barbara and the young refugees. Adolescents or their parents may be in doubt as to where to turn. If a young person is involved in further education contact with a counsellor could be available, providing a natural basis to think about further help and how it may be obtained. We saw how Barbara's parents were helped to think about a way to find a solution through contact with other parents with similar problems.

We have provided a list of useful organisations at the end of the book. It is probably clear from the text itself that the writers would favour seeking help, when necessary, from professionals with an approach which pays careful attention to the actual experiences and feelings of the young people concerned, rather than giving automatic advice.

Step-parents and step-children

It may be difficult at times for parents to accept their child's choice of partner, but it can also happen that their child may have very mixed feelings about a parent's choice of a new partner. Cecily, as mentioned previously, had lost her mother in a car accident when she was eighteen. She had understandably not been very sociable for a period of time, but when she was twenty, she had become more outgoing again, and had had a steady boy-friend for some months. She had assumed that her father would never wish to remarry after her mother's death. She was still living at home when father started going out much more and eventually informed her that he intended to be married to Mavis, a woman a little younger than himself, and who had two children of primary school age. Cecily's first response was one of indignation. How could he? What would her mother have thought? Although what she conveyed was a wish to preserve her mother's memory, there were also more complex and difficult feelings which Cecily had to recognise when she realised that her father was determined to go ahead with the marriage.

Since her mother's death, Cecily had become used both to feeling that she was 'the lady of the house', running the household for her father, her brother and herself very efficiently. She also found it difficult to adjust to the idea that when she herself was moving in the direction of getting engaged to be married, her father might be doing the same. Last, but not least, having had to battle with her mixed feelings about the birth of her brother in her early childhood, she might have felt that she would not again have to put up with the unwelcome arrival of new children in the family. Cecily's father was entitled to be firm about his wish to remarry, but at the same time, fortunately, was able to show understanding of Cecily's complicated feelings.

The problem of accepting children coming from a previous marriage into the family is one which can also be very disturbing to children of divorced or separated parents. This is very likely to happen when a parent of children of the age group we are discussing remarries.

Cecily was confronted with a particularly difficult experience. She began to feel that the house which she had been running - and that she had looked after so efficiently - was being invaded by Mavis and her children. Toys and video games were strewn around in the living room and sometimes crisps, eaten during children's television programmes, were dropped, stepped on and ground into the previously immaculate living room carpet. Cecily found it quite upsetting when Mavis took matters in hand and cleared up after her children by using the vacuum cleaner. At the same time she found it difficult: she did not wish to clean up after the children, but resented Mavis taking over. Cecily felt that the house had become child centred. The one sunny corner in the garden where she used to sunbathe was now occupied by a large climbing frame which Mavis and the children had brought with them.

Cecily was beset by a range of complicated feelings. She had already given some thought to moving out with her boyfriend Rodney. Now she was partly motivated towards the move by her own feelings of displacement and wanting her own place. It was still difficult for her to relinquish the house which she felt she had properly taken over from her mother. She was resentful because she felt hurried into a move before she and Rodney were quite ready to set up home together. She went through a period of doubt and uncertainty, but could not bear to stay with her father and Mavis, especially after she heard that Mavis was pregnant. The thought of this future half-brother or sister was too much for her and she very quickly moved in with Rodney. The new environment contrasted painfully with what she still experienced as her own home, as Rodney only had a bedsitter with cooking facilities.

Potential parenthood and abortion

Soon after the move, Cecily felt confronted with a heartrending choice. She missed a period and thought that she was pregnant. What should she do? She didn't think that she and Rodney really felt ready to become parents at this stage in their lives and seriously considered having an abortion. Rodney himself was very divided, as he felt that at some time he would like to be a father. As they were talking the matter over, he rather took Cecily by surprise by saying that she might have forgotten to take the pill so as not to feel outdone by Mavis in having a baby. Cecily was somewhat taken aback and was at first rather resentful about Rodney's remark, but, on reflection, could see that he might have a point. The practical logistical problem of not having a suitable place to bring up a child increased Cecily's resentment about Mavis having taken over the spacious house of her childhood. Fortunately she proved not to be pregnant, but before finding this out Cecily went through a time of considerable stress and turmoil.

In Cecily there was still a competitive little girl who might have wished to have become pregnant in rivalry with Mavis. On the other hand, there was also a thoughtful and quite mature twenty-year-old, with good memories of her mother and her mothering. She had it within her to become a good mother, but, at this time, the rivalry with her father's new wife was so intense that these feelings may have predominated. This is an instance in which it would have been difficult to have a definitive answer as to the wisdom of having an abortion.

In this age group, young people may make up their minds about issues such as abortion without wanting to talk it over with their own parents. On other occasions parents might be very much called upon to help with thinking about such a decision. Early in this book we referred to Yvonne as someone able to make thoughtful independent choices. When she became unintentionally pregnant, Karl, the father, a fellow music student, was about to return to his country to complete his musical studies there. Yvonne felt that it was very easy for her to approach her parents and talk with them about the difficult decision that she had to make: should she have an abortion, should she keep the baby, knowing that she would be a single mother? Yvonne's parents knew that it was not straight advice that was sought by their daughter. They provided, as they had done on many other occasions during her life, the type of receptive attention that helped Yvonne to think about her predicament. Yvonne decided to keep the baby, having given very careful consideration to the responsibility she would be taking on as a single parent. She was also encouraged by knowing that her own parents were behind her in making the decision and were clearly willing to stand by her and help in whatever way they could.

The relationship between Yvonne and Karl had not lasted very long but, on the whole, was a happy one with a shared love of music. The baby had not been planned, but once it was conceived, Yvonne found greater resources for parenting within herself than Karl was able to find within himself at that time. She realised that the responsibility of keeping the baby was hers. She had hoped to keep in friendly contact with Karl, thinking that this might matter later to the baby, but this sadly did not prove to be possible.

A young woman may at times feel a wish to have a baby which does not arise from her most mature self. It may spring from desires of long ago, when, as a little girl, she may have wished for her dolls to come alive so that she could have a baby just like mother. Some lonely girls may want to have a baby as company, with a frequently forlorn hope that this will provide some kind of comfort for the child within themselves, unaware of the huge, adult task involved in its care. Such states of mind are very different from an adult motivation related to bringing up children and facing all the hard work involved, including a great deal of anxiety, sleepless nights and an infinite range of responsibilities lasting up to the age range we discuss in this book.

A new generation

Shortly after setting up home with Roy, Patsy became pregnant and the couple then got married. The tension between Roy and his parents had diminished considerably after the decision to marry was announced, but although contact with Roy's family was more frequent and the tradition of joint Sunday lunches was resumed, the relationship between Roy and his parents was not quite the same as it had been previously.

When little David was born, his birth affected family relationships very profoundly and very positively. When Roy had set up house with Patsy, his parents found it difficult to relinquish the task of trying to bring up their son according to their principles. The new perception of Roy and Patsy now having become parents themselves brought a different quality into the relationship between the generations. Roy's parents could recognize that bringing up David was the task of his parents, Patsy and Roy, and, while making themselves available to help in any way that they could, they were able to keep their own views to themselves. They in fact came to appreciate a certain relaxed quality in their relationship with David, which they had not experienced as fully in bringing up their own children. It is true in fact that, like most grandparents, not being directly responsible for the way in which their grandchild was being brought up lent to the relationship a certain lightness of heart.

The relationship between Roy and his parents had been weighed down by grievances which had been difficult to relinquish. Roy could not forgive them for the lack of full recognition of his independence; they could not forgive him for breaching their standards. The sense of grievance on both sides seemed to fade away under the impact of shared joy at David's birth. The parents felt a sense of continuity in that David was the name of Roy's father; had the baby been a little girl Patsy would have wished to call her after her own mother. Whether or not this very concrete way of representing the continuation of life in the next generation takes place, grandparents may well be grateful to their children for what they experience as the gift of a grandchild in whom they feel that some spark of their own life is continued.

> . . . a child, more than all other gifts
> That earth can offer to a declining man,
> Brings hope with it, and forward-looking thoughts.
>
> Wordsworth: 'Michael'

FURTHER READING

Box, S. et al. (ed), *Crisis at Adolescence: Object Relations Therapy with the Family*. Jason Aronson Inc., New Jersey and London, 1994.

Copley, B., *The World of Adolescence: Literature, Society and Psychoanalytic Psychotherapy*. Free Association Books, London, 1993.

Salzberger-Wittenberg I. et al., *The Emotional Experience of Learning and Teaching*. Routledge and Kegan Paul, London, 1986.

Shakespeare, W., *Romeo and Juliet*

Tolstoy, L.N., *War and Peace*

HELPFUL ORGANISATIONS

Brook Advisory Services, Birth Control Clinics, 153A East Street, London SE17 2SD
Helpline (24 hours) 0171 617 8000
Centrepoint, 2 Swallow Place, Bewlay House, London W1R 7AA 0171 629 2229
The Eating Disorders Association, Sackville Place, 44 Magdalen Street, Norwich NR3 1JU
Helpline (9am–6.30pm Mon–Fri) 01603 621414
Youth Helpline (4–6pm Mon, Tues, Wed) 01603 765050
Release (Criminal Legal Drug Service), 388 Old Street, London EC1V 9LT, 0171 729 9904
Helpline (24 hours) 0171 603 8654
Samaritans (Head Quarters), 10 The Grove, Slough SL1 1QP 01753 532713
For local helpline numbers check the inside front cover of local telephone directories.
The Standing Conference on Drug Abuse (SCODA), 1–4 Hatton Place, Hatton Garden, London EC1 8ND 0171 430 2341
Freephone 100 and ask for Freephone Drug Problems
Young Minds, 22a Boston Place, London NW1 6ER 0171 724 7262
Helpline (9am–5pm Mon–Fri) 01345 626376
Young People's Counselling Service, Tavistock Clinic, 120 Belsize Lane, London NW3 5BA 0171 435 7111 ext. 2337
A self-referral service in London for young people by previous telephone appointment only.

UNDERSTANDING YOUR CHILD

ORDER FORM FOR TITLES IN THIS SERIES

Send to: Rosendale Press Ltd, Premier House
10 Greycoat Place, London SW1P 1SB

Price per volume: £5.75 inc. post & packing

Understanding Your Baby by Lisa Miller	..... copies
Understanding Your 1 Year Old by Deborah Steiner	..... copies
Understanding Your 2 Year Old by Susan Reid	..... copies
Understanding Your 3 Year Old by Judith Trowell	..... copies
Understanding Your 4 Year Old by Lisa Miller	..... copies
Understanding Your 5 Year Old by Lesley Holditch	..... copies
Understanding Your 6 Year Old by Deborah Steiner	..... copies
Understanding Your 7 Year Old by Elsie Osborne	..... copies
Understanding Your 8 Year Old by Lisa Miller	..... copies
Understanding Your 9 Year Old by Dora Lush	..... copies
Understanding Your 10 Year Old by Jonathan Bradley	..... copies
Understanding Your 11 Year Old by Eileen Orford	..... copies
Understanding Your Handicapped Child by Valerie Sinason	..... copies
Understanding 12–14 Year Olds by Margot Waddell	..... copies
Understanding 15–17 Year Olds by Hélène Dubinsky & Jonathan Bradley	..... copies
Understanding 18–20 Year Olds by Gianna Williams & Beta Copley	..... copies

Total amount enclosed: £. . . . .

Name . . . .

Address . . . .

. . . . Post code . . . .